SUMMARY OF

Girl, Wash Your Face:

STOP BELIEVING THE LIES ABOUT WHO YOU ARE SO YOU CAN BECOME WHO YOU WERE MEANT TO BE

By

RACHEL HOLLIS

DENNIS BRAUN

Disclaimer

This book is a summary and meant to be a great companionship to the original book or to simply help you get the gist of the original book. If you're looking for the original book, kindly go to Amazon website, and search for Girl, Wash Your Face by Rachel Hollis.

Table of Contents

EXECUTIVE SUMMARY

Rachel Hollis' "Girl, Wash Your Face" carries one main theme throughout its chapters: that what becomes of your life, ultimately, is up to you. You have so much power to dictate the outcome of your life, but without trashing all the untruths you've been fed so far (and even the ones you fed yourself), there's no harnessing the potential of that truth.

Hollis teaches women how to overcome these falsehoods by sharing her personal experiences. Each chapter begins with her telling readers how she once patterned her life after a particular lie. She ends each chapter with a couple of tips that helped her overcome said lie. Some of the lies she tackles border on self-worth, the true source of happiness, the root of gossip, and many more.

Actually, reading Hollis' book feels very much like hearing from a friend. It's the kind of book you probably want to curl up and get comfortable with. What's more, she gets practical by telling you exactly how to go about conquering those fears and taking charge of your destiny.

CHAPTER 1: The Lie: SOMETHING ELSE WILL MAKE ME HAPPY

Key Takeaways:

- *There is no flawless life. It simply doesn't exist*

- *Only you can create your own happiness*

- *Surrounding yourself with positivity is key to creating your happiness*

- *Stop the comparison game. You are you alone*

The other day, while enjoying some playtime with my boys, I legit wet my pants. It wasn't like that one time in camp when I went all the way and had to cover up by spilling the contents of my water-bottle down my pants, but it was still slightly humiliating. Nobody noticed this time but of course, I did. Interestingly, this occurrence was a testament to the childbirth road I had gone down three times. Nothing stays the same after you house a baby in and push it out of your body. If you've been in my shoes before or understand how it feels, you're probably smiling right now. But it's okay if you're scrunching up your face in slight disgust, because that's how I know you don't know what I'm talking about.

Anyway, there I was, jumping on a trampoline and grateful for the breeze going through my shorts. Less than thirty minutes later, my Facebook status was updated with pre-posted images of me testing different fancy dresses for the Academy Awards. My husband's job affords me the opportunity to attend fancy events, get glammed up and what-not. Not unexpectedly, I got a lot of 'oh-your-life-is-so-perfect-and-glamorous' comments on the pictures, and I was there thinking how many people had no idea I just wet myself while jumping on the trampoline in our backyard.

There is absolutely nothing glamorous about my life and there's nothing patronizing about that fact. I really am not flawless- as a wife, mother, friend, boss, or Christian. I mess up like any other human being. I have battles like every other person. I need you to understand this before moving on in this book. I need you to understand that even though I run a Lifestyle website and proffer solutions on how people can live better lives, I'm far from perfection, and I'm far from it every day. I need you to understand that none of us is perfect. None! We're all figuring this life thing out together.

Every day, I determine to become a better me than I was yesterday, because I know it's up to me. Yet, even with this knowledge, some days are better than others. Sometimes I make real, obvious progress, and on other days, I flunk and just look forward to the next day- another chance at being better. The signals we get from society are mostly unhealthy and sadly, that is what reigns supreme in mot minds. We've been told we need to have it all together or be completely non-existent. I get a lot of notes and comments from my readers and followers, and a lot of women have just given up altogether. You're basically just going through the motions of everyday life while you're devastated.

Life should be lived, not endured. Sure, there'll be challenges here and there. Sometimes you'll feel miserable about one thing or the other. But these times are not meant to constitute the essence of your life. They should not be what your life is about. You have this one life and you have power over it. You can overcome challenges and come out stronger and better. You can! And you know what? This is not a license to become egoistic or godless. However, you have to realize that if you're upset and disappointed with the life you live now, you should be held responsible.

I don't mean when you're depressed or grieving. I mean when you're resigned to living an unfulfilled life that you'd rather not think about. There are happy people; people who delight in their lives even though they know it's not perfect and even when they face challenges. They're happy because they take responsibility and act. I am one of such people, and that happiness is what people see when they tell me how flawless my life looks.

My life is not flawless. As a matter of fact, I grew up in a troubled home and was raised by dysfunctional parents. As though that wasn't enough, my older brother committed suicide in my first year of high school. Basically, I grew up way beyond my age. My brother's death filled me with the determination to make a better life for myself. I did all I could to get far away from my troubling background, eventually moving to Los Angeles before I was 18. I was so sure my contentment lay anywhere away from home, and at first, when I got to L.A, I felt I was right. I couldn't differentiate the euphoria of novelty from true happiness. Soon enough, I realized that moving away from one place to another does not guarantee happiness. Rather, your conscious choice is the ultimate deciding factor.

The following tips helped on the journey to locating my happiness in myself alone. You should try them out too:

- I stopped measuring myself- successes, achievements, failures and what not- against any other person or the ideal 'ME' I had in my head. Instead, I focused on simply being better than yesterday's 'ME'.
- I made space in my life for only positive people and things. I realize this sounds really cliché but I also know it's true.
- I recognized the things that my spirit finds joy in and did them constantly. If something or someone drives away the peace from you, then maybe you should move away. You *can choose* to move away.

CHAPTER 2: THE LIE: I'LL START TOMORROW

Key Takeaways:

- *Breaking promises should not be a habit, not even to yourself*

- *You don't have to commit to everything. It's okay to say no*

- *Start by seeing through the small promises you make to yourself*

- *Be sincere with yourself*

The sheer number of failed diets, marathons, workout sessions, etc. that I've missed attest to the fact that I was once a chronic procrastinator. I was very good at signing up for things, talking up a storm about how I'd do this and that and eventually not doing them. Unfortunately, many of us are guilty of the same trait. Yes, even the media is more dedicated to suggesting how to recover from a slip-up than how not to slip up in the first place, and to be honest, slipping-up is only human after all. But when it becomes a defining trait and our pledges are as good as nothing, then we need to look inwards.

Some months back, I went out to dinner with a couple of friends, and even though we ended up running late, I still ran some miles on our treadmill when I got home. When one of my friends whom I'd gone to dinner with saw my Snapchat post of the treadmill session, she couldn't believe it, and she said as much in her text. I replied, telling her I didn't want to renege on the promise I had made to myself and she totally did not understand why I couldn't just reschedule for the next day. She saw no big deal in my breaking a promise to myself.

But here's the deal. You wouldn't trust someone who was always going back on their word, would you? Well, even though you may not know, your subconscious takes note of your broken promises and concludes that you cannot be relied upon. Your subconscious can determine when you truly want to achieve something or if you're just all talk and no action. It simply looks at your existing database to see how you've fared on past 'resolutions'.

For instance, the last time you promised yourself to run 10k and went only 4? Well, your subconscious remembers, and whenever you make that promise again, it will remind you just as you approach that 4k. You'll start to get really tired after that mark and if you're still bailing out on yourself, the most you'll do after 4k is a few miles. If you're however serious about keeping your word, you'll push beyond that precedent and achieve your goal.

I experienced this myself, and if I had not been resolute about achieving my goal, today, I would still be addicted to Diet Coke. That was the first time I would make a promise to myself and not break it, and from then on, keeping every other promise came much easier. My subconscious had gotten the signal that I was not joking around. My diet coke training came in handy when I decided to run my first marathon and when I decided to write my first novel.

I know firsthand how easy it is to shelve commitments made to yourself, and I also know how such actions can shape your entire life. Keeping the promises you make to yourself also influences your life, this time positively. When you make the conscious choice to keep your promises, you'll commit to fewer things. You won't make promises carelessly anymore and you'll be able to give yourself to those things that really, truly matter.

Doing these things helped me and they can help you too:

- Start with the small stuff. Before committing to that diet, try drinking water equivalent to half your body weight every day.
- Stop saying yes to everything. Just because something is admirable doesn't mean you should commit to it. Save your yes for those things you know you can pull off and that are of utmost importance to you.
- Do a truthful audit of your action in the past month and see how you've fared with keeping to your promises.

CHAPTER 3: The Lie: I'M NOT GOOD ENOUGH

KEY Takeaways:

- *Your self-worth does not lie in your achievements*
- *Therapy does you good*
- *Listen to your body. It knows what it needs*
- *You come first*
- *Seek leisure*

For years now, I have been aware of the fact that I'm a workaholic. Most folks have no idea of the seriousness in that description. They have no idea it is just as bad as any other addiction out there. It's an addiction because a workaholic feels constrained to work overly even when she doesn't have to. That was me, or more accurately, is still me to some degree. I feel like I'm better than I was but even now, I feel some form of compulsion to be able to meet up with all the responsibilities I shoulder. I still work till I'm physically drained and cranky.

The fact that I absolutely love and excel at what I do is partly responsible for my workaholic disposition. I love the fact that my small-girl dreams have grown into something big with the help of an amazingly creative team. When I'm at work, I 'get it'. It's unlike me at home when I can be disheveled and feeling incompetent. So, expectedly, I tilt towards work.

If that was the only reason, then it'd be a less complicated issue, wouldn't it? But of course, it's not. There's the fact that as the last child of the family, I had older parents who were preoccupied with many things, like their chaotic marriage. So for the most part, I didn't have their attention unless I scored an achievement. In other words, I got to feel cherished only when I did something good. Sadly, that pattern was somehow ingrained into my subconscious and served as the basis for my actions as an adult. My self-worth was tied to a compulsion to work and work I did. I was always doing something; never stopping enough to rest or celebrate an achievement. I did not see how much I was hurting my health as well as my family.

Work was my crutch. Once, when I was nineteen and afraid of an impending break-up, I threw myself maniacally into work until my body shut me down with facial paralysis. I was depressed and more self-conscious than ever about my appearance. Yet, the breakup I was trying to prevent eventually happened. Worse still, the paralysis came back, interestingly while on a romantic getaway. It was then that the doctors discovered that this condition was being brought on by excessive stress. I was like many women out there- giving all of yourself and not taking care of yourself.

Our bodies are very good at communicating to us when they're being overworked. Unfortunately, most of us are not very good at listening. So when the body's had enough, it does something drastic to get your attention. Just recently, I developed Vertigo. It was so bad that I was beginning to constitute a danger to myself and those around me. I couldn't figure out what could be causing it and I was resigning myself to a lifetime of dizziness when I heard of a specialist. During the session, he simply told me my vertigo was a reaction to severe stress and his solution? Do nothing!

I can't begin to explain how horrified I was at his suggestion, and that was when it hit me. I was very good at giving women tips on how to live better, healthier lives and there I was breaking one of the cardinal rules. I failed to look after myself. That was the turning point for me. I stopped working those insane hours and forced myself to take rest periods where I just sit, doing nothing. It wasn't easy, but I took it one day at a time. I engaged in leisure that made my heart glad. I immersed myself in therapy. I studied the scriptures from which I got the assurance that my achievements were nothing compared to my confirmation as a loved child of god. I learned to celebrate my achievements and not fret over what's next. I learned to accept that even without all those achievements, my world would still be alright.

These tips also helped out, and I'm hoping you'll find them useful too:

- **Invest in some therapy**. This helped me uncover the root of my workaholic disposition. Without that knowledge, any other solution i might have applied would only be misinformed and misdirected.
- **Go out of your way to seek happiness**. Invest some of that energy you pour into work into doing things that delight and relax you. You'd be surprised what wonders taking time off can do for your work-life.
- **You come first**. If you're not first on your scale of preference, something is wrong. You cannot give what you're not, so unless you're healthy and

happy, you're not going to be of much help to anyone and anything.

CHAPTER 4: The Lie: I'M BETTER THAN YOU

Key Takeaways:

- *We need to stop putting each other down*

- *When you point one finger at another person, three others point right back at you*

- *Behind every hurtful word is usually a deeper insecurity*

- *You can't overcome a bad habit without determination*

- *Your way is not the only way*

The one time I made fun of someone was in High School and it still irks me till this day. Not so much because I was talking smack about a girl who shaved her toes when I was also doing the same thing, but the fact that there is a tendency for many of us to find pleasure in ripping other women apart. And just as teenage me was acting largely from a place of insecurity, our mean words as adults are usually fueled by something similarly trivial.

Do you somehow feel better with yourself when you talk down another woman? Or do you feel less imperfect when you ceaselessly pick at another woman's faults? Sadly, no.

Most of the time, the flaws we point out in others are a reflection of the ones other folks point out in us. It's not cool. There is no way it's alright to speak negatively abut another, even if it is in their absence. The earlier we recognize the significance of the words we speak- the earlier we recognize the sway they hold over lives- the earlier we'll see the need to change our ways.

Trust me, this is something we need to deal with. As much as I know how messed up it is to condemn other people, I still find myself falling into it every now and then. Recently, I was on a plane with a family that included a very ill-mannered child and it took a while for me to realize that I was already judging the mother. When I came to my senses, I could think of a million and one reasons why a mother who looked absolutely miserable might be finding it hard to control a difficult four-year old.

The fact that condemning another woman comes almost instinctively does not mean we should endorse it. In fact, we need to do away with it ASAP! Judging keeps us from building or sustaining a community, something that is necessary if we are to succeed as women. We need to stop tearing each other down or trying to outdo each other in an imagined, frivolous competition of life. First things first, you need to stop kidding yourself (if you already are) that you don't judge or think yourself to be better than the next woman. Judging can come in subtle ways, sometimes not even involving a single word. One look or tilt of the head from you can signify a lot more than some words would.

The next thing to do would be to acknowledge that your way is not the only way. Stop feeling like you know all there is to know about anything or that anyone who holds a contrary opinion is 'wrong'. As you may have guessed, there is no topic that illustrates this better than religion. For most of us, any religion asides ours is wrong. Not sure what your religion holds as a fundamental principle but in mine, it's to love our neighbors- no attachments or conditions. Sadly, we often mix up judgment and criticism with accountability. The latter cannot function in a place of contempt or hatred and this is where unhealthy comparison thrives.

In all my years of catering to women's needs through my lifestyle website, I have come to discover that the foremost need of women is community, kinship, interaction. But we can't achieve this without shedding all the weight that comes with criticism and rivalry. Instead of sniffing out our differences, we need to start looking for common ground and focusing on that. We need to look past each other's religions or fashion sense and focus on the individual.

I fought this lie by applying the following:

- **Surround yourself with the right crowd**. You spend so much time with women who take pleasure in tearing others down and you'll be headed that path soon enough. Surround yourself with women who are more concerned with building each other up.

- **Watch yourself**. Let's face it. If you're not determined about shaking off this bad habit, then no amount of persuasion will make you. Stay conscious of your reactions towards other people and check yourself when you're beginning to stray. It also helps to force yourself to see something good in that person you're so quick to tear apart.

- **Get to the root of the matter.** Find out what really makes you so quick to rip out another person. Usually, it's one insecurity or the other lurking behind all those cruel words.

CHAPTER 5: The Lie: LOVING HIM IS ENOUGH FOR ME

Key Takeaways:

- *Love yourself first. Don't lose yourself while loving another*
- *Don't hesitate to walk away when you're being treated poorly*
- *You are not alone*

My first 'falling in love' experience came at the age of nineteen. He was one of the visitors that came calling on my boss and I was swept away the first time I saw him. Completely inexperienced and naïve about dating and relationships, I did not see anything wrong with my whirlwind emotional reaction to someone I was meeting for the first time. Not even after he spent our entire first date talking about himself was I disenchanted.

My young age was an issue for him, and he told me as much. But I was already seeing myself married to this man, and I refused to think age could stop anything. I spent many nights with him, and in my mind, he was my boyfriend. Unfortunately, the feeling was not mutual and he made that clear with his words and his actions. Yet, I willingly discarded my ideals and justified his actions with one reason or another.

This was a long time ago but I still remember my experiences like it was yesterday. What hurts me more is that many women are still going through this today: allowing a man to treat them awfully. I'm hoping my experience will help you be truthful with yourself and make better choices. I went through a whole year of bowing to his every whim and explaining away his demeaning treatment of me, and even now I weep for the girl I was. I wish that girl had not been so insecure and lacking in confidence that she'd been willing to settle for scraps. I wish someone had been there for me as a guide through the 'love' terrain.

I was so damaged that my self-worth was tied to his love and acceptance. When he broke up with me, I shamelessly wept, pleading with him not to dump me. Still terribly heartbroken, I got a voicemail from him the next day. And it was in that moment that I had an epiphany. For the first time, I saw my experiences for what they really were and was horrified at who I'd become. With a newfound clarity of mind, I called back and told him I was done allowing myself to be treated badly and that he was never to call me again.

The next morning, there he was on my doorstep. My husband. That signaled a new beginning for our love and the man he is today is nothing like that man who hurt me so deeply. We must remember however that not all stories will end like this. Whatever the case, never allow yourself to be treated like dirt.

My sincere expectation is that my story will help you to be truthful with yourself. Accept when you're in a relationship that undermines your worth and get out of there. Don't hesitate to walk away from anything unhealthy. You are not alone. Many other women have gone through this, and many are still going through it. At the end of the day. It's up to you. Will you continue accepting less because you love someone or will you stand up and fight for your self-respect?

These will help:

- **Get a listening ear.** It's easy to look at your relationship with rose-colored glasses when you're in love. It's easy to gloss over the unpleasant truth, so have someone else you can talk to; someone who has your back and won't be scared to tell you the truth.

- **Be Informed**. It would have been helpful if I'd had someone to give me a heads-up on the basics of love, dating, and relationship.

- **Take the outsider's point of view**. Imagine narrating every detail of your relationship to an outsider. If you imagine their thoughts won't exactly be *"what a healthy relationship!"* Then you should do an audit of that relationship.

CHAPTER 6: The Lie: NO IS THE FINAL ANSWER

Key Takeaways:

- *Convert a "no" into something that would profit you*

- *Own your dreams*

- *See the good in the bad situations*

There are people who are hardworking, do not joke with time management and are even talented but do not still hit it big. This is because they succumbed to whatever hurdles came their way. Being rejected or getting a "no" doesn't mean giving up on your dreams. "No" helps you go back to your drawing table, trace where you got it wrong and prepare adequately for the journey. It helps you find out how else you can achieve your dreams since the method you're currently adopting is not working out. On your low days, see it from the point of view that something good will eventually come out of it. We see life and the things that happen to us through our own filters, our own biases and our own lens. So decide to always find the good in the bad.

Usually, you live life today based on what you have gone through in the past days. If nothing has ever fallen into place for you in the past, you would keep living with the perception that nothing ever works for you or you are even cursed. So when you receive a "No", it's nothing more than your usual. However, a change of mindset can turn things around for your good.

So, figure out your dream(s) and identify them. At some point or the other, you have never really thought of those dreams aloud and possess them because of panic or fear of failure. Note your dream and then admit your fears about the dream. If you keep the panic in, they would grow and you would unconsciously nurse them. People give up on their dreams for different reasons: for some, it could have been because someone who holds a measure of importance in their lives told them it would not work out for some reasons.

By the way, during those low days when you feel like you have done absolutely nothing worth praising in your life while it seems like every other person is achieving something here and there, cry if you need to. Then wipe your tears, freshen up and brace up for your next move. Remember that achieving your dreams is a matter of life and death because you either choose to actually live and not exist or die before you are dead. It is important that you do some soul searching; you dig deep and then nurse those dreams and potentials inside you. Durable things take time to build so enjoy the process. It is more about how you eventually see yourself and how you have grown at the end of the day. Possess your dream.

- Ignore the expert opinion; don't be rude but stick to your dreams.
- Sometimes when you encounter a hurdle, change your course but still be on your way to the desired destination.
- Be specific about your goals and put it up where you can see it.

CHAPTER 7: The Lie: I'M BAD AT SEX

Key Takeaways:

- *If you desire to have a better sex life, you would be better at sex*

- *Appreciate your body; it would build your sexiness*

You could be bad at sex but here are a few ways to go from being an amateur to being an expert:

- Change your perspective about sex. If you keep considering what else you could be doing asides having sex that particular time, you'd eventually not do it. So think of it as something amazing.

- Identify exactly what is affecting your sex life and talk to your partner about it.

- Figure out ways to spice things up in bed. It doesn't have to be something harmful; it just has to be a harmless thing that helps you enjoy sex better or turns you on faster.

- It is also important to love your own body. You would have more confidence while having sex. You cannot enjoy sex if you keep wondering if your butt is appeasing enough or if your tummy isn't looking too big. So find something that is sexy about your body and highlight it. You can also tell yourself your butt looks great!

- Don't fake your orgasm. Be determined to reach orgasm right when you have to start sex.
- Dig deep and know what turns you on. You and your partner could try to explore to find out.
- Deliberately decide to have sex as frequently as you can. Practice makes perfect. When you keep getting better at sex, you'd want to have more sex.

CHAPTER 8: The Lie: I DON'T KNOW HOW TO BE A MOM

Key Takeaways:

- *Take care of your baby and don't neglect yourself*
- *Motherhood is from within, it is not very difficult*
- *Avoid media that makes you feel like you are not measuring up*

A lot of panic is attached to being pregnant and the early stages of motherhood. It is even possible for you to dislike your spouse a few weeks after the birth of your child. It is not entirely strange. You may feel like you are not caring for your baby enough or that your spouse is not helpful enough in helping you care for your baby. You may not feel connected to your child or you're so conscious of making mistakes that you eventually miss out on the little joys of watching your baby smile or even changing his diaper.

You do things like you're treading on egg shells, you are too careful that you end up not getting it right. Don't try to copy or measure up to the standard you see in adverts or on the media. Just put your heart to feeding your baby, cuddling your baby, making sure his wet diapers are replaced and keeping your baby warm. It is not rocket science. As you are taking care of your baby, don't neglect yourself too.

Motherhood is innate so don't panic that you would mess up because it is in you. Do your best and leave every other thing to fall into place for you. Here are some ways to figure it out:

- Belong to a group of like minds or that are facing similar "I'm-a-new-mom" situation as you. It is easier for you to relate, share ideas and rub minds. That way, you also won't feel like you're the only person doing it wrong.
- Avoid perfect motherhood images or videos on the internet, if not you'd keep chasing the ideal and you won't create what is suited for you and your baby. Figure out what exactly is making you feel like you are not doing your best and stay away from it.
- Do not stay at home; it is easier for you to slip into self-pity when it's just you and the baby at home. Go out, take a walk, listen to hip-hop.
- Share your burden with someone. It would give you some help.

CHAPTER 9 The Lie: I'M NOT A GOOD MOM

Key Takeaways:

- *Be the best you can be in raising your children*
- *There is no "correct" way to raise your child, as long as your child turns out okay*
- *Don't beat yourself because you are a working mom*

It could be challenging trying to balance your career with being there for your children or even trying to be like all the other moms you know. Don't try to be like those other moms, rather work with a schedule or a plan that suits you and your children. Don't topple over trying to please everyone, be the best at the little things you can do to improve your children. Other people maybe perfect but sometimes being perfect is overrated. Maybe you don't know how to handle some things or you don't know how to make home-made cookies for bake sales but maybe that is also okay.

Do your best and don't hate yourself when you forget your child's open day. Identify the things about your children and school that you do the best and emphasize those things. Do that and be the best you can be and the things you need to work on, keep improving them. There is always one thing that makes you question your ability or how great you are as a mom but then do your best and leave the rest. There is no best way to parent your child and don't try to impose stuff you see other people do if it won't work. Being a parent is a mix of the good, the bad and the ugly but the goal is to care about them and yourself.

Once in a while, take a break so you don't just slump one day. Do something else asides being a mom and get refreshed. Go on a date, do your mani-pedi, go swimming, see a movie. It will help your mood and disposition and your children will even notice it when you get back home. It'd be easier for you to teach your children to be cheerful when you are cheerful. Also, stop weighing yourself, your kids, your family or mode of parenting against other moms, other kids, other families and other seemingly-perfect mode of parenting. Always strive to be a better version of yourself not a carbon copy of another mom, also teach and groom your children to be the best version of themselves. If you're a working mom, love yourself like that.

You have to pick your battles wisely. You can still chase your dreams and balance it with being a mom. Don't struggle about your decisions as a mom because it doesn't look like what everybody else is doing. Do your best, please your kids, make your kids happy, do those little things they want you to do like making their hair or giving them a peck before they go to school or singing them a special song before bedtime. Care for your children but don't become irritable while doing it. Figure out the things that strikes you as your "I'm proud to be a mom" and "I love my kids" moments and do them often. Be unique, it doesn't necessarily have to be what half of the moms in your daughter's class take as their own happiest mom moments. You can learn from other people but if it does not suit you, discard it. Again, the beauty of the whole thing is that there is no hard and fast rule to being a mom.

- So, look at the beautiful and amazing things about your kids and be proud of yourself as a mom but if there is none to be proud of or the bad outweighs the good, seek help.
- Get to know those other moms you're pitting yourself against. They also have where they're screwing up and you would see that everything is

not always the way they seem. Also, create time for them.

- Don't spend all the time working or being on your laptop or phone; give your children piggyback rides, build Lego castles with them, make baby faces at them.

CHAPTER 10: The Lie: I SHOULD BE FURTHER ALONG BY NOW

Key Takeaways:

- *It is never too late to accomplish your dreams*
- *Not everything you want is meant for you*
- *Trust your growth process and celebrate your successes*

Sometimes, you make a bucket list of plans and then you check it off the checklist. You even have deadlines attached to this list and then when you do your checking, you discover that you haven't achieved half of what you set out to do at a particular time. So you probably don't like growing older because you feel that you haven't achieved enough and time is short. Anyway, that is a huge lie. It is never too late to do anything as long as you are still breathing. Why not think of the presence of the little things you have and not focus on the absence of the things you have done.

Don't beat down yourself too hard, cut yourself some slack. It is harder to snap out of it because it is an internal war raging in your body. And then you eventually say it too much that you eventually believe it, and they become your truths, they form the basis on which you live your life. But then, know that things would happen when they are supposed to.

You don't have some things yet because you can't handle the pressure it brings just yet or you don't have the capacity to accommodate it yet. So, take a chill pill. Or maybe those things you even want are not right for you; they are not meant for you. Everything that is happening now is preparing you for your next big moment. The setbacks, the disappointment, they are all working for you to help you handle your next achievement better.

Rather than feel sad because you haven't achieved enough, put in your best into what you have right now and watch it bloom, grow and flourish. Have trust in your process and cherish it. Believe that everything will eventually fall into place; because there is only so much you can do as a person. If you knew tomorrow, you won't need faith. But since you don't know tomorrow, you definitely need faith.

Most times, the greatest and most amazing things that happen to you were never really on your bucket list; they came along because you did your best and trusted the process of growth. So, calm down. Just make sure you are the best at what you are doing currently. Be happy with all the things you have achieved. Don't dwell on them but celebrate those moments because they help you up during the low days. God knows exactly what He is doing and even though you may not eventually reach where you think you should be, you are exactly where you are meant to be. And you would end up exactly where you are supposed to go.

- Appreciate yourself and come up with a list of the things you have achieved, even the littlest things. It definitely helps your psyche and shows you that you have the ability to achieve even more.
- Make sure you talk to someone; a burden shared is half solved.
- Set goals but do not attach unrealistic deadlines to them.

CHAPTER 11: The Lie: OTHER PEOPLE'S KIDS ARE SO MUCH CLEANER/BETTER ORGANIZED/MORE POLITE

Key Takeaways:

- *Don't ignore the chaos around you*

- *Take a breather and address the chaos with a clear head*

Accept disorder so that you can find tranquility. Everyone has their own definition of chaos and we try to manage it in three ways: some people choose not to notice or attend to the chaos. You may pretend it doesn't exist but then the ripple effects will eventually haunt you. You may also decide to fight it by doing what you can to let out the pain but it does not necessarily mean you are solving the problem or addressing the situation.

But usually when you don't address the situation directly, you'd end up losing the battle you chose to fight. You may also select the option of letting the chaos swallow you and you get submerged in it. You focus on it so much that you see nothing else and then you forget to keep your head above the water.

All these coping mechanisms seem fine but just a very short while before the chaos eventually catches up with you. Trying to fight is like believing that you are in charge of everything or you let everything happen. You are not in charge of other people's actions so you can only do your best. What to do is to accept the disorder so you can see the beauty in all the stress. The way you deal with the chaos now depends on you as a person.

Take a pause and look at the situation, find the good in the bad. Know the fruits of the Spirit and know which one you need per time. Take a breather so you'd be able to address the situation with a clear head. Share your burden and seek support. Also learn to receive help from people, it would save you stress. It'd also give you a little time for yourself.

- Looking at your issue from a fresh perspective could also help.
- You need friends who are in your similar situation; they would uplift you and you can discuss your situations with them.

- You have to sort which issue is most important to you and attend to it.
- Identify your happy place and chill there when you have issues. Just live and work through your chaos.

CHAPTER 12: The Lie: I NEED TO MAKE MYSELF SMALLER

Key Takeaways:

- *Do not belittle yourself*

- *Do not cower from your dreams. Change your world*

Do not play or see yourself as small. It's okay to have big dreams and chase them hard. It is okay to want to change the world with the big things you are going to do. Never see yourself or anything you do as small. Don't be uncomfortable to discuss your dreams or state your achievements just because it will affect other people. If you do it too often, you would even start to believe it and start thinking and acting small. Do not deny yourself of the life you truly deserve just because it might step on other people's toes. Be comfortable in your own skin. Don't live in fear of your own self.

Recognize that thing God has put in you that makes you unique and maximize it. Change the world with your plans, don't hide from yourself. Do not be afraid from your dreams and woman, you own your world. If you dream it, you can surely have it. Don't limit your dreams in anyway and definitely, don't look down on yourself.

Know that you cannot always get on everyone's good side and not everyone would be approving of you or your choices. Be at your best and stop bothering yourself about what everyone else thinks. You owe no one an explanation! You choose your personality and you can decide to be outspoken about it. Soak up knowledge from other sources – feed your mind on things that pertain to the areas of your life you need to beef up.

CHAPTER 13: The Lie: I'M GOING TO MARRY MATT DAMON

Key Takeaways:

- *Be precise about your future*

- *Your dreams push you to survive the hard times*

Being specific about your dreams help you achieve them faster. Single out a huge part of your success and see it in intricate details. Listen to people that pump you till you are full of ideas and surround yourself with motivational content. Being specific about what you want would help you make decisions and take huge steps that would take you exactly where you have thought of. Let your dreams be real to you; let them be concrete. When your dreams are real to you, when things get stormy and rough, your concrete dreams remain the anchor you have to hold on to. It helps you concentrate on where exactly you want to be.

Take note of your dreams on pen and paper. Then imagine how you would look in your dream home, what the color of the cushion would be, how your children would look like in their school uniforms and so on. Concentrate on these dreams and you can decide to have visual aids around you to keep pushing you. They even help you get through the annoying and even sad days, that way you push yourself harder to achieve those dreams.

You can think of getting really close to the person you admire from a distance or maybe even a celebrity, going on vacation with this celebrity or the object of your secret fantasies, or just something big that fits your own personality. As stupid as it sounds, these dreams help you up your game and give you strength to push further to dreams every passing day.

It is important that you note your dreams on pen and paper or even on your notepad. Then "confess" them, say those specific dreams to yourself every time. The more it rings in your sub-conscious, it is only a matter of time until they become your truths and they eventually happen. Don't forget the visual aids because they would go a long way in you giving life to your fantasies.

CHAPTER 14: The Lie: I'M A TERRIBLE WRITER

Key Takeaways:

- *Refuse to give half a hoot to what other people think*
- *Not everyone would accept your piece of art no matter how seemingly amazing it is*
- *Put your work out there for yourself and no one else*

You may have done something you think is a very fantastic job and you're happy with all the good feedback you are getting. And then suddenly, from nowhere, someone says something not too cool about your work. Then you feel dejected. Hey, hear this, "Someone else's opinion of you is none of your business". Let that sink thoroughly into your mental faculty. For people who give two hoots about what other people think, you really have to start living by the mantra above.

When you conceive an idea and birth it, you know all the effort that you put in it and you know you have done your best. The idea you have conceived is something that has burned in you for years that you just have to execute it. It may have been the most amazing thing you have brought to life but you cannot make everyone accept it. That people think of it as bad does not make it bad. It's not like you would ignore constructive criticism that would definitely make you grow but accepting that your creation is not cool because one person or persons thought of it that way is not good for your psyche.

It takes a certain amount of strength to come up with a creative piece. So don't let anyone beat you down with their words. So put your ideas and work out there because you, yes you created it and put in your very best. It is worth the risk of people not getting your point. Just do what you have to do, everyone does not have to like it.

So, do something and don't even bother to care what people think about it. Do what you are doing for yourself and not for anyone else or money for that matter. Do things that give you joy, it sharpens your creative mind.

CHAPTER 15: The Lie: I WILL NEVER GET PAST THIS

Key Takeaways:

- *You are stronger than think, you just have to draw strength from within*

- *Don't let your past define you*

Some very terrible, ugly things happen to you and they color the way you wade through life. But you have to be strong, reach deep and since it didn't kill you, let it make you stronger. When you eventually get through it, appreciate those dark moments and find the good that came out through it. So when other tough times come, you know you can live through it because you have survived worse.

It's not healthy to treat your hurt as if it doesn't exist but it would help you so much if you would accept it and let it forge you to be stronger. Things could happen to you but don't let them characterize the course of your life. It's not easy to lose a loved one but have it in mind that you would definitely get through it. Don't let it drown you and the very thing that makes you you. Keep your head afloat and try as much as possible to make it to shore. Everything happens for a cause and the thing which has caused you so much hurt will eventually shape the things that would give you joy later.

Go for psychotherapy if you need to, seek help from other people who you can call your confidants and talk to them about it, think about it as much as you can until it has no power over your mind anymore.

CHAPTER 16: The Lie: I CAN'T TELL THE TRUTH

Key Takeaways:

- *Don't breed your hurt*

- *No matter how many times you fall, stand up*

The bad things dominate you when you empower them. Even when things happen, believe you would definitely be alright at the end of it all. Beauty will eventually come out from your ashes. Don't see yourself as someone who has been torn apart by circumstances; instead see yourself as someone who keeps getting up every time you stumble, going at the very thing you have envisioned for yourself even if circumstances keep dragging you back.

Admit the things you are going through and it will be easier for you to deal with them. Share your problems with people who have also gone through hard times. Find a tribe who has found themselves in exactly the same situation as you. It would help you understand and go through it better.

CHAPTER 17: The Lie: I AM DEFINED BY MY WEIGHT

Key Takeaways:

- *Treat your body right; stay healthy*

- *You don't have any excuse to punish your body, it's not worth it*

You could be a stress eater who cures or ignores pain by eating a lot. Don't be at odds with your body; don't let it be what characterizes you. It could be difficult for you to stay skinny even when you are fat and all you just want to do is eat. You have many things buried inside of you and you have to exhibit these things and change the world because of them. Care for your body by eating right, doing workouts and taking water at appropriate times. Your size does not characterize you but the effort you put into making sure your body is as good as new characterizes you.

We all have excuses for why you aren't taking care of your body but it doesn't matter. Those excuses no matter how weighty are trifle when weighed against the punishment and dishonor you are doing your body. You have the option of living above your past experiences or not; you have the option of taking your pain out on your body or not; you have the option of remaining in dark place or not but don't ever believe that staying in that dark phase of your life and maltreating your body is what you are worthy of.

Just stay hale and hearty, you don't have to be fat or thin. If you really want to start loving and appreciating yourself, you have to start taking care of your body. Staying healthy or adopting weight loss programs are not very difficult, just resist the temptation not to stress eat, adopt a workout routine that suits you and look for another way to deal with issues asides food.

Discard all negative thoughts and start replacing them with positives. Say these positive things to yourself; the more you say it, the more you become it. Be careful of what you feed yourself through the media; avoid pages or pictures that make you start feeling low about your body. Take time to plan and strategize how you want to adopt healthy eating habits; if you want to start exercising (plan ahead) or Join a fitness program, prepare a meal timetable to be able to monitor what you eat.

CHAPTER 18: The Lie: I NEED A DRINK

Key Takeaways:

- *Adopt healthy coping mechanisms*

- *Your problems do not vanish just because you distract yourself from them*

- *Know your triggers*

You have probably believed that anytime you are stressed out, the only way to solve your problem is to drink. You have probably believed it so much that you now actually depend on drinking to get through tiring days. It is very easy to get addicted to drinking. Drinking is a temporary answer to not feeling the pain because when the alcohol wears off, your issues have definitely not vanished, they are right there and you have less strength to face it because of the alcohol you have consumed.

You have to decide to build strength from whatsoever issues comes your way and by building strength it means facing issues head on and coming out better from all the pain. So when those kinds of things reoccur, you already know how to get through it; you don't have to rely on alcohol or food or even porn. Think of other healthy ways to cool of such as exercising, swimming, praying, crying, hanging out or maybe even doing your mani-pedi.

Don't ignore the issues you are facing by diverting your attention to all those temporary fixes that will eventually do more damage than good. You would have to face issues, learn and grow from them. Be knowledgeable about what triggers your bad habits, it would help you avoid the "drink". Admit your weakness and be aware of it, it would help you stay off it. Try hard not to see the things that trigger your bad habits e.g. alcohol and porn websites.

CHAPTER 19: The Lie: THERE IS ONLY ONE RIGHT WAY TO BE

Key Takeaways:

- *There is no correct way to live*
- *Viewing things from other people's lens gives you a broader worldview*

We all have our beliefs and we have all been raised in different ways. But if you decide to stay rigid for the rest of your life, you would not acknowledge the beauty that is in the diversity of race, culture, religion, beliefs and value systems.

You may lose out on the best friend you would have had if you decide not to break free of the homologous ways and beliefs with which you were brought. You may lose out on the companionship that would have been beneficial to you if you decide to only move with people who have the same beliefs as you. That is too boring and ordinary, you would not learn because you would think the way you do things is the only and best way there is.

It is the difference and uniqueness in the world that makes it beautiful to explore. There is no best or correct way to be one thing. You do not have to change your value system because you want to accommodate others, let everyone hold on to their own belief system. The point is not to see others as wrong or look down on others just because they are not doing things the way you would do it.

You could change your community or get a different circle of friends. Admit that you have once said derogatory things to people who don't think the way you think and then choose to change. You can ask questions from these "different" people and not just assume that you have all the answers.

CHAPTER 20: The Lie: I NEED A HERO

Key Takeaways:

- *You are your own greatest motivation*
- *Yearn for change and go for it*

Once you set out to do something, you can. You don't need anyone to be your superman; you can be your own superman. For everything you do, you put your own effort in it no matter how minute or huge it is. It was all you! So, you are definitely your own champion. The tiny quirks and perks are what makes you you, so glory in it. People can definitely help you and contribute to your success but if you do not put in any effort, it is going to be zero. You can do all things through Christ gives you strength.

Stand up for yourself. Don't wait for anyone else to stretch out their hands to pick you up, rather dust yourself and pick yourself up. There is no hard and fast rule about being your own champion. Yearn for change and look deep for the strength that is in you and the one that God has deposited in you.

Don't just want or wish for change, yearn for it and work towards getting it done. You know the change you want as it differs from person to person. Don't wait for anyone because the only person that can do it is you. Stop moping around, stop maltreating your body, stop beating yourself up. Get up and do something. Remember a girl's gotta do what she gotta do.

Made in the USA
Lexington, KY
22 January 2019